Cohen

EGYPTIAN
MYTHS AND
LEGENDS

ALL
ABOUT
MYTHS

Fiona Macdonald

Raintree

Chicago, Illinois

© 2013 Heinemann Raintree
an imprint of Capstone Global Library, LLC
Chicago, Illinois

To contact Capstone Global Library please
phone 800-747-4992, or visit our website
www.capstonepub.com

Edited by Nancy Dickmann, Adam Miller,
and Claire Throp
Designed by Jo Hinton-Malivoire
Original illustrations © Capstone Global Library,
Ltd., 2013
Illustrations by Xöul
Picture research by Hannah Taylor
Production by Victoria Fitzgerald
Originated by Capstone Global Library, Ltd.
Printed and bound in China by Leo Paper
Products, Ltd.

16 15 14 13 12
10 9 8 7 6 5 4 3 2 1

**Library of Congress Cataloging-in-
Publication Data**
Macdonald, Fiona, 1958-
  Egyptian myths and legends / Fiona Macdonald.
    p. cm.—(All about myths)
  Includes bibliographical references and index.
  ISBN 978-1-4109-4972-1 (hb)—ISBN 978-1-4109-
4977-6 (pb) 1. Mythology, Egyptian. 2. Legends—
Egypt. I. Title. II. Series: All about myths.

BL2441.3.M36 2013
398.20932—dc23   2012017692

Acknowledgments
We would like to thank the following for
permission to reproduce photographs: © The
Trustees of the British Museum p. 37; Alamy
Images pp. 9 (© dbimages), 16 (© INTERFOTO);
Corbis pp. 12, 22, 36 (Sandro Vannini); Getty
Images pp. 5 (Ethan Miller), 8 (IC Productions);
Shutterstock pp. 6 (© Natursports), 13 (© Goran
Bogicevic), 14 (© John Said), 21 (© Lisa.S), 40
(©Nestor Noci); SuperStock pp. 4 (Image Asset
Management Ltd), 7, 20, 23, 28 (DeAgostini),
15 (Holton Collection), 17 (LatitudeStock), 39
(Universal Images Group), 41 (JD Dallet); The Art
Archive pp. 33 (Egyptian Museum Cairo/Dagli
Orti), 38 (Dagli Orti); Werner Forman Archive
pp. 26, 32 (E. Strouhal), 27, 29 (Egyptian
Museum, Cairo).

Background images: Shutterstock (©Kamira),
(©Kokhanchikov), (©Serg64), (©Fine Shine),
(©Dudarev Mikhail), (©AridOcean), (©Fedor
Selivanov), (©Dudarev Mikhail), (©Inc),
(©Lukiyanova Natalia/frenta).

Cover photograph of the Viscera Coffin of
Tutankhamun reproduced with permission of
Getty Images (Ethan Miller). Cover graphic:
Shutterstock (© Martin Capek).

The publisher would like to thank Professor
Mark Smith of the Faculty of Oriental Studies,
University of Oxford, for his invaluable assistance
in the production of this book.

Every effort has been made to contact copyright
holders of any material reproduced in this book.
Any omissions will be rectified in subsequent
printings if notice is given to the publisher.

Disclaimer
All the Internet addresses (URLs) given in this
book were valid at the time of going to press.
However, due to the dynamic nature of the
Internet, some addresses may have changed,
or sites may have changed or ceased to exist
since publication. While the author and publisher
regret any inconvenience this may cause readers,
no responsibility for any such changes can be
accepted by either the author or the publisher.

CONTENTS

Did you know?

Discover some interesting facts about Egyptian myths.

WHO'S WHO?

Find out more about some of the main characters in Egyptian myths.

MYTH LINKS

Learn about similar characters or stories from other cultures.

WHO WERE THE ANCIENT EGYPTIANS?

The ancient Egyptians lived in North Africa long ago. They created a rich, powerful civilization that lasted for over 3,000 years, starting around 3100 BCE.

Egyptian people were farmers, potters, weavers, painters, builders, designers, and engineers. They studied math and medicine, and made careful observations of the stars. They explored new lands. They trained a strong army, and conquered nearby peoples. They liked stories, music and dancing, nice clothes, and big families. They thought that life was good, and hoped to enjoy it forever.

MYTHS AND MAGIC

Egyptians worshiped many different gods. They believed in magic, and told myths to answer important questions, such as "What is a good way to live?" or "What happens after we die?" This book tells some of the best-known myths from ancient Egypt.

MYTH LINKS

Egyptian artists portrayed the sky as a giant goddess with a star-covered body. Her name was Nut, and she stretched over Earth to protect it. Every night, Nut swallowed the Sun (shown here as a red ball), then gave birth to it in the morning.

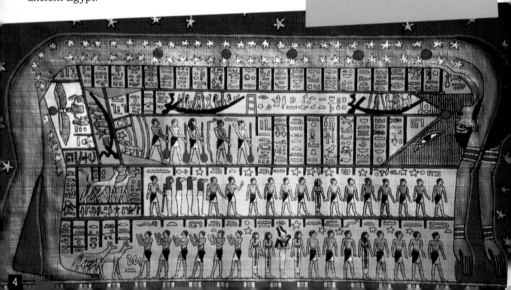

For how to pronounce Egyptian names, see pages 42–43.

This ancient Egyptian man, Pharaoh Tutankhamen, gazes out from a mummy coffin made over 3,000 years ago. Masks like these helped to preserve and protect the mummy underneath.

MYTH LINKS

Myths are stories with meanings. They have been told by people from many different civilizations, all round the world. Myths can't be proved like science or math, but they can tell us truths about good or bad behavior, relationships, ideas, and feelings.

TREASURES
FROM THE PAST

We can still admire many treasures made in ancient Egypt. The most famous treasures include lifelike statues, huge temples, and fabulous golden jewelry found in pharaohs' tombs.

EVERLASTING GOLD

The Egyptians clearly loved beautiful objects. But these treasures also had hidden meanings. For example, Egyptians described the skin of the gods as being made from gold. Gold did not rust or decay, and it also symbolized the Sun and its rays. If people or mummies wore gold, then it might help them live forever.

TIMELINE OF ANCIENT EGYPT	
c. 5500 BCE	First farms are built beside the Nile River.
c. 3000 BCE	Egyptians begin to write using hieroglyphs.
c. 2589 BCE	Great Pyramid is built at Giza.
c. 2500 BCE	Sphinx is built at Giza.
1327 BCE	Tutankhamen is buried in the Valley of the Kings.
332 BCE	Alexander the Great, from Greece, conquers Egypt.
30 BCE	Last pharaoh, Cleopatra, dies. Romans conquer Egypt.

■ The pyramids at Giza were built between 2589 and 2503 BCE, as tombs for Egypt's pharaohs. Their shape may have been inspired by a myth about how the world began (see pages 10–11).

MYTH LINKS

Both the ancient Egyptians and the Maya people of Mesoamerica linked cats to the Sun. They described how a big, fierce, shining cat, Jaguar-Sun, prowled across the sky every day, from east to west.

MYTH LINKS

Cats killed mice and rats that ate the Egyptians' food and threatened them with starvation. Because of this important role, cats became symbols of good in Egyptian myths. Cats were sacred to the goddess Bastet. When they died, they were made into mummies. Egyptians also gave mummified cats as gifts to the goddess.

IN THE BEGINNING

Who made the world? Who made the gods? How did the first living beings appear? Egyptian creation myths provided several different answers to these questions.

Many creation myths featured water. This was not surprising. Most of Egypt was desert, but the mighty Nile River, the longest river in the world, flowed through the country from south to north. All year round, it provided freshwater. Then, from June to September, it overflowed its banks, flooding the land and spreading thick, black mud. Egyptian farmers grew grains, fruit trees, grapevines, and other crops in this mud.

Did you know?

Egyptian farmers divided the year into three seasons:
- *Akhet*: The Nile flooded the land.
- *Peret*: Farmers plowed fields and planted seeds.
- *Shemu*: Farmers harvested ripe grain, fruits, and vegetables.

Houses along the Nile are built on dry, rocky land, safely above the floods.

GIFT OF THE NILE

The river brought life; without it, the Egyptians would have died. No wonder they called their land "the gift of the Nile." They worshiped Hapy, the generous green (or blue) god of floodwaters. He was king of the river, and father of all the fishes; his friends were frog-goddesses—and crocodiles!

Egyptian artists sometimes portrayed Hapy with a bulging stomach full of food.

MYTH LINKS

The Egyptians welcomed the Nile floods, but, in many other countries, water was feared. In Scotland, myths told of the terrible Each Uisge (say: Eck-Ooshkya), a flesh-eating water-horse that grabbed passersby, dragged them under the water, and then ate them!

New land, new life

Before the world began, there was nothing. No day, no night. No trees or mountains. No houses or cities. No men, women, or children. No Sun, no Moon, no stars. Nothing, except darkness.

But there was the god Ptah. He is a creator, and he brings into being eight small eggs. No one really knows what happens next. Perhaps Ptah swallows the eggs and gives birth to them. Perhaps he transforms into water—an ocean that covers Earth.

But look! The water is moving! The eggs have hatched! And what are these creatures slithering toward us? Four look like men, but they have frog heads. Four have women's bodies, slim and graceful. But their heads are like snakes. They have forked tongues.

Slowly, as if waking up for the very first time, the eight mysterious creatures rise to the surface of the water. All at once, they are free—to leap and splash and swirl and swim and dive and dance together. Now we can see that they are couples, one frog, one snake. Each pair of them has a name, which tells us where they come from or what they are. Kek and Kauket are "darkness"; Nu and Naunet are "water"; Heh and Hauhet "force" or "infinity"; Amun and Amaunet are "hidden power." They are gods; they are monsters; they are life!

They dance, laugh, and sing, and their energy causes an explosion. It is the beginning of the world we know.

But what happens next? Some stories say that the frog gods—Kek, Nu, Heh, and Amun—merge to form a powerful black bull. The snake goddesses—Kauket, Naunet, Hauhet, and Amaunet—come together to form a beautiful black cow. The cow and bull produce a beautiful lotus flower in the lake.

And look! The flower is opening. Inside is the glorious, golden, shining sun god, in the form of a child. He will reign in the sky, sending his rays to warm and welcome everything they touch. Ancient Egypt's world has been born. Ra, the sun god, has risen.

CONTINUING CREATION

The god Khnum was linked with the Nile. When potters used the clay brought by its floodwaters to make bowls and dishes, they thanked Khnum for it. He became the god of all craft workers.

One myth tells that Khnum shaped the first men and women from clay, on his potter's wheel. Then he filled the muddy little creatures with mysterious "ka" (life force) and set them free.

THINKING IS DOING

Another myth describes a different kind of creation. Ptah, one of the Egyptian creator gods, spent years thinking deeply. Then he forced all his thoughts out of his heart and up into his mouth. They became words and poured out into the world, turning into people, animals, and all kinds of living creatures.

MAGIC AND MYSTERY

Myths said that the sun god Atum sneezed, and—achoo!—created Shu, god of the air. Then he spat—splash!—and water goddess Tefnut was born. Together, Shu and Tefnut produced Nut (the sky) and Geb (the earth)—and that's how the world began.

Khnum is shown here with the head and horns of a mighty ram—signs of his life-giving power.

Did you know?

The Egyptians believed that the heart, not the brain, was the home of all thoughts, ideas, and feelings. Hearts also stored memories, and a record of each person's good or bad actions.

After the end of the ancient Egyptian civilization, the knowledge of how to read and write hieroglyphs was lost and forgotten. It was only rediscovered in the 19th century.

GODS AND GODDESSES

If you were an ancient Egyptian, you might have doubts or worries. Would your crops grow well? Would your children be good? Would the Nile floods bring enough water? But you'd feel absolutely certain about one thing: there were gods all around you.

Egyptian people believed that powerful beings controlled this world and the next. There were gods or goddesses keeping watch in the sky above and haunting the underworld, home of the dead. There were gods for pharaohs and their queens, and gods for poor, ordinary people. There were also gods, like Osiris, that had died and been reborn.

WHO'S WHO?

The goddess Hathor was gentle, kind, and nourishing. This statue shows her with ears like a mother cow, symbol of love and caring. Hathor was also pictured as the band of stars streaming across the sky. Today, astronomers call these stars the Milky Way.

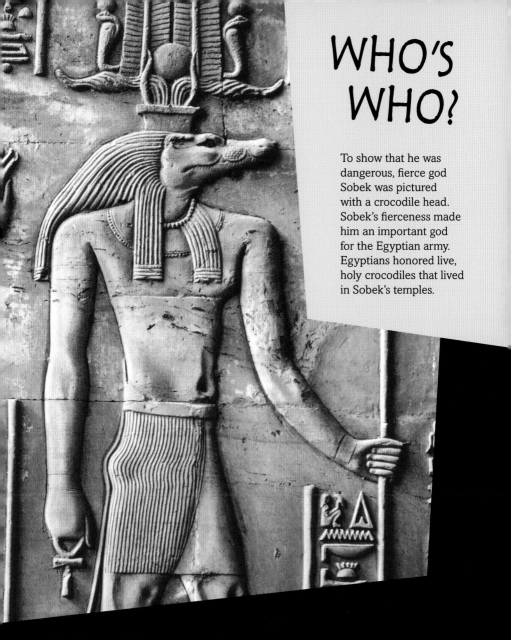

WHO'S WHO?

To show that he was dangerous, fierce god Sobek was pictured with a crocodile head. Sobek's fierceness made him an important god for the Egyptian army. Egyptians honored live, holy crocodiles that lived in Sobek's temples.

SUPERHUMAN

The gods were awesome, mighty, and mysterious. They could sometimes appear on Earth, but they were not like people. The Egyptians gave gods names, such as "he who is far-seeing," but did not know what they looked like. Instead, they used images to show the gods' special powers. For example, they pictured Thoth, god of writing, with a bird's head and a long, slim beak that looked like a pen. Sometimes gods and goddesses were shown with a sun disc above their heads.

GODS GREAT AND SMALL

The greatest god in Egypt was Amun-Ra. As his double name tells us, he was two gods joined together.

Amun was everywhere, invisible, all-powerful. His name meant "the hidden one." Ra was bright, dazzling, clearly seen by all. He was the king of the gods, lord of the Sun. He sailed across the sky in a shining golden boat, bringing life, light, and energy.

■ This gleaming silver statue shows Amun-Ra as a god and a king. The crown with tall feathers was a sign of Amun. The round golden sun was the sign of Ra. The braided beard could only be worn by Egyptian royalty.

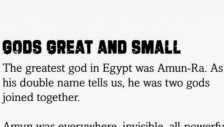

Did you know?

Around 1350 BCE, Pharaoh Akhenaten ordered all Egyptians to worship a new sun god, called Aten. He had Amun-Ra's name and picture removed from as many places as possible. Priests at Amun-Ra's temple were furious. As soon as Akhenaten died, they made sure that Amun-Ra was honored as king of the gods once again.

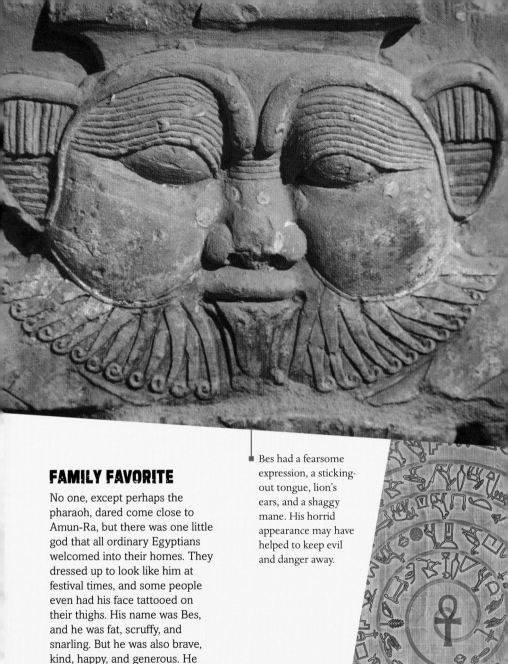

FAMILY FAVORITE

No one, except perhaps the pharaoh, dared come close to Amun-Ra, but there was one little god that all ordinary Egyptians welcomed into their homes. They dressed up to look like him at festival times, and some people even had his face tattooed on their thighs. His name was Bes, and he was fat, scruffy, and snarling. But he was also brave, kind, happy, and generous. He protected mothers and children. He kept poisonous snakes away.

Bes had a fearsome expression, a sticking-out tongue, lion's ears, and a shaggy mane. His horrid appearance may have helped to keep evil and danger away.

Terror of the lion-goddess

Before kings existed, Egypt was ruled by Ra, god of the Sun. But he was getting old and tired, and the Egyptians disobeyed him.

Ra summoned some of the other gods, to ask their advice. "The people of Egypt are plotting against me," he told them. "Shall I kill some of them? Then the survivors would fear and obey me."

The other gods thought that this was a good plan. One of them suggested, "Let your Eye go and kill them for you!"

Now, the Eye of Ra was a very weird and wonderful thing. It helped him see hidden mysteries, but also went off and had adventures on its own. It could take many forms, and this time, Ra agreed that it could take the shape of a goddess. She went down to Earth and killed many Egyptians. Ra was pleased that she had done what he asked.

But in solving one problem, Ra had created another. The more people that the savage, lion-headed goddess Sekhmet killed, the more blood she wanted. If no one stopped her, she would wipe the Egyptians out entirely! Then who would be left to worship Ra?

But Ra had an idea. A good one! He sent for sacks of red ochre from the desert, and ordered all his servant girls to brew lots of beer. When it was ready, Ra mixed the ochre into the beer, turning it red like blood. He poured the red beer onto the land—thousands of jars of it, until the fields were flooded. Then Ra and the other gods waited to see what would happen.

Sekmet was on her way to kill more people. But before she arrived at the town, she came across the fields of red beer. Just as Ra hoped, Sekhmet stopped, thinking that it was blood. Ra watched excitedly as she drank…and drank…and drank. Soon she was too sleepy and full of beer to even think about killing humans.

The Egyptians were grateful that Ra had saved them from Sekhmet. And Ra? He was happy at last.

Did you know?

Egyptians believed that a few real animals were "living images" of their gods. This statue shows an Apis bull receiving an offering. Bulls like these were specially chosen by priests as the image of creator god Ptah. They lived in Ptah's temple, and were said to foretell the future. They were given magnificent funerals when they died.

FESTIVALS AND OFFERINGS

Where did Egyptians go if they wanted to worship? They said prayers at home to household gods like Bes, and to Taweret, the lumbering hippo goddess who protected pregnant women. They took part in community festivals, when statues of gods and goddesses were carried through the streets or floated on decorated boats along the Nile River. Priests made offerings to the gods in magnificent temples, and asked for favors in return.

The temple of Amun at Karnak was built between 2055 and 1650 BCE. The best workmen and the finest stone were chosen to create it. It is decorated, inside and out, with images of gods and pharaohs, and scenes from myths.

A HOLY HOUSE

Temples were homes for the gods. Like royal palaces, they were huge, with lakes and gardens. Many also had schools for scribes. Hidden away, in the holiest part of the temple (called a shrine), stood a splendid statue of the god or goddess. Only priests and members of the royal family were allowed to enter.

Did you know?

Priests cared for the statues of gods and goddesses as if they were alive, feeding them, washing them, dressing them, and getting them ready for bed every night.

SONS OF THE SUN

Egyptian kings, known as pharaohs, were much more than rulers. They were seen as living links between people and the gods. Pharaohs called themselves "sons of the Sun," and a few even claimed that their mothers were magically married to sun god Amun-Ra, as well as to their real human husbands.

At home in their palaces, pharaohs wore magnificent jewels and held splendid feasts to impress important visitors and honored guests.

WHO'S WHO?

Some pharaohs had many wives, and even more children. Most pharaohs were men, but a few ambitious women managed to win power. The most famous was Hatshepsut. She wore royal clothes, like a male pharaoh, including a false beard.

GOVERNMENT BUSINESS

Pharaohs fought against real-life dangers, such as invaders. Myths said that they had god-like powers as leaders and warriors. In peacetime, pharaohs founded cities, encouraged trade, and built magnificent palaces, temples, and tombs.

NAMED FOR THE GODS

Each living pharaoh had five names. Two of the most important were "Son of Ra" and "Horus." They might also be given the name of a third god, Osiris, after they died. Horus was god of the sky. He was shown with the head of a hawk, a bird famous for its "all-seeing" eyes. Osiris was ruler of the underworld, kingdom of the dead. He was shown as a mummy in bandages.

Did you know?

Pharaohs had many religious duties. As chief priests, they led festival processions and temple ceremonies. Egyptians believed that these rituals helped keep Egypt safe. Without them, demons and other evil creatures might destroy the kingdom. This statue shows a pharaoh making offerings to the gods.

The lost jewel

How do you amuse a man who has everything? That was the problem facing Djadja-em-ankh, chief scribe at the palace. His master, Pharaoh Sneferu, was bored. Bored, depressed, and bad-tempered. How about a party? An elaborate feast? No—that would not do. The pharaoh needed something new, different, and exciting.

The palace had a beautiful garden. In that garden, there was a lake surrounded by flowers. It was summertime; the afternoon was hot, the weather was sultry. What, thought the scribe, could be more refreshing than a boat trip on the lake? Especially if the rowers were 20 pretty women!

Picture the scene: the lake is cool, the women are singing, the pharaoh is smiling (hooray!). "Ah! This is the life…" he says to the scribe.

But then: "Aiiiiieeee! Aiiieeee!" One of the rowers is screeching. What's the matter? Why the fuss?

Ah! She's lost the beautiful turquoise jewel she was wearing in her hair. It's fallen into the water! The pretty woman stops rowing. She just sits and shrieks. She won't obey the pharaoh when he tells her to get moving. He's looking very angry! Who can calm him—and comfort her?

The scribe is wise, he knows magic. Raising his arms, he chants a secret spell. Slowly, and very, very strangely, the lake waters roll away. Then they rise up in a huge watery wall—and look, there's the turquoise jewel, stuck in the mud they've left behind!

Quickly, the scribe picks it up. As he hurries back to the boat, muttering more words of magic, the water-wall collapses with a great swoosh and swirl and gurgle. Soon the lake is as calm and still as if nothing unusual had happened.

And the pharaoh? Well, this has certainly livened up his day. He leads his trusty scribe into the palace, and they share a splendid feast together.

MAGIC, MONSTERS, AND MEDICINE

Today, we would be very surprised if our doctors chanted magic spells, or said that our illness was caused by demons. But the Egyptians believed that evil forces were at work in the world. These took the shape of monsters and demons, or appeared as dangerous animals, such as snakes and scorpions.

MYTH LINKS

Some monsters were good, not evil. But their superhuman size and strength still made them terrifying. The Great Sphinx was part lion, part man, part sun god. Egyptian pharaohs were often portrayed as sphinxes to show their power.

This painting shows the god Ra as a giant cat, killing Apophis, an evil snake monster.

DEMONS

Egyptian myths told of two different types of demons. Some were unquiet spirits, including people who walked in their sleep and dead bodies that could not rest in their tombs. Others—even more dangerous—were monsters from the underworld.

These demons brought sickness, accidents, and bad luck. Egyptians used medicine, religious rituals—and magic—to fight against them.

A SECRET WEAPON

Egyptian people also used magic to harm real-life enemies. They would write a name on a piece of pottery, then crush it underfoot. Egyptians thought that as the name disappeared, its owner's mind or body would weaken.

WHO'S WHO?

Sometimes good, but often evil, Set (also known as Seth) was god of chaos. He was shown with a long snout and strange square ears. Sometimes he had a man's body, but he might appear as an "unclean" dog, pig, or donkey.

These strange demons stop those dead souls that are unworthy from entering the underworld. The good have nothing to fear from them.

SIGNS OF LIFE

The Egyptians used magic to fight against demons, evil gods, and restless mummies. They waved wands or wore amulets. Wands were carved with images such as lions (signs of strength) or scarabs (signs of life). Mothers made magic circles with them to protect sleeping children, chanting spells or saying prayers as they walked around and around. They hoped no demon would dare step inside the circle they had made.

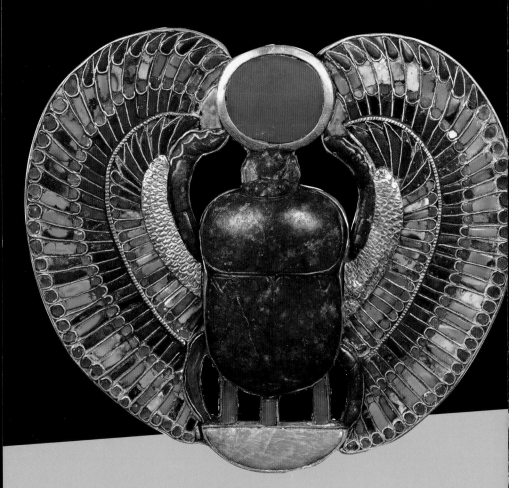

MYTH LINKS

The scarab (dung beetle) was a symbol of Khepri, one of the forms of the sun god. When Egyptians saw how baby scarabs hatched, mysteriously, from balls of dung, they hoped that they might also be reborn one day. This amulet made for a rich Egyptian shows a scarab beetle ready to fly. Its front legs hold a glowing ball, a symbol of the Sun.

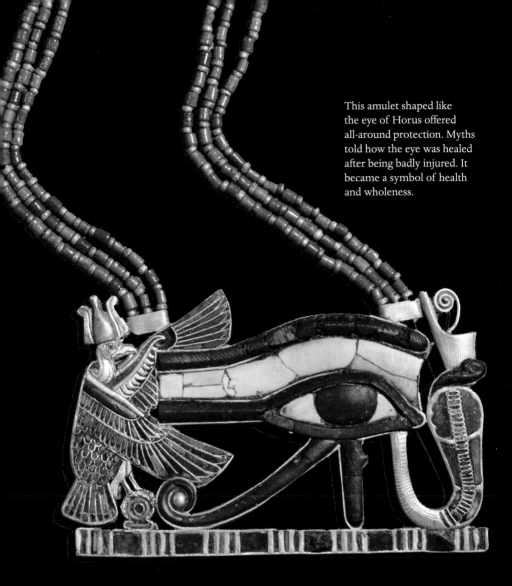

This amulet shaped like the eye of Horus offered all-around protection. Myths told how the eye was healed after being badly injured. It became a symbol of health and wholeness.

LUCKY CHARMS

Amulets were shaped like kindly gods, such as Bes, or sacred animals, such as Apis bulls. Other amulets copied powerful symbols, such as "ankh," a hieroglyph that meant "life." Mummy wrappings often included a heart-shaped amulet, to prevent the mummy's own heart from being taken away, or a "djed-pillar," a little model of Osiris's backbone. That was meant to bring strength—and the hope of new life.

Burial chambers were guarded by four magic bricks, each decorated with a special symbol. The bricks were carefully arranged at the four main points of the compass: north, south, east, and west. Egyptians believed they kept evil spirits away.

The prince and the Sphinx

Sometimes it's hard to be a favorite son. That's what young Prince Thutmose thought, every time his brothers were horrible to him. He couldn't help it if his father was always saying things like, "That's my boy!" or "I'm proud of you!"

Naturally, Thutmose's brothers were jealous. Of course, they plotted against him. They all thought that they had a better right than him to follow their father as the next pharaoh.

Thutmose began to spend more and more time away from the royal palace. He often drove his chariot into the desert. One day, sweaty and exhausted, he sat down in the shade of a very large boulder. Straight away he fell asleep, and began to dream...

The boulder turned into a head. The head was like a man—or perhaps a god. The head had a body. But that was like a lion. A strange light glowed in its eyes, with the power and majesty of the Sun.

The creature stood up, and shook itself. It towered over Thutmose, who was no bigger than one of its fearsome claws.

"I am the Sphinx," the monster boomed. "Pharaoh Khafra made me. But that was over a thousand years ago, and now I am buried."

"If you set me free from this desert sand, I will help you in return. I'll make sure that you become pharaoh, and that your reign will be glorious."

Thutmose opened his mouth to speak, but no sound came. He stepped forward toward the monster...

There was a deep roar, followed by an almighty flash from the Sphinx's shining eyes. Then the world went black; Thutmose fell to the ground.

We don't know how Thutmose managed it, but he did clear the sand, and proudly put a carved stone slab between the monster's paws to tell the world what he had done. The slab is still there today. And he did become pharaoh, as Thutmose IV, and ruled from 1400 to 1390 BCE.

EVERLASTING LIFE

The ancient Egyptians loved life, but they saw death all around. Compared with today, there were few old people. Most people felt lucky to reach their 40th birthday.

MAKING A MUMMY

The Egyptians believed in life after death, but it was not easy to achieve. First, a body had to be preserved as a mummy. Then rituals had to be performed to provide the dead with other things needed to survive in the next world. These things included a name, a shadow, ka (life force) and ba (form in which they moved from one world to the next). Without all these, a dead man or woman had no hope of everlasting life.

MYTH LINKS

Inner organs removed from mummies were placed in pots called canopic jars. These had tops shaped like four mythical beings, the Sons of Horus. Each one protected a different organ: lungs, stomach, intestines, and liver.

A human ba was invisible. But Egyptian artists liked to show it as a beautiful bird, free to fly between the living and the dead.

Mummy-making was a smelly, messy business, so workshops handling dead bodies were always located out of town. Once a mummy was completed, it was wrapped in bandages with amulets tucked inside. Then it was ready to be carried to its tomb.

To make a mummy, the body's brain and inner organs (except the heart) were removed. Then it was put in natron (salt) to dry, filled with rags, and coated with resin (gum). The whole process took 70 days.

MYTH LINKS

The world's oldest mummies come from Chile and Peru. They were buried in the desert between around 7020 BCE and 1720 BCE. They were probably made because ancient South American people worshiped their ancestors, and wanted to show respect to their dead bodies.

Love finds a way

Wise Isis. Isis, the winged beauty. Isis, who found a way to heal her husband and help Egyptians find everlasting life. Isis, who made the first mummy.

This is her story.

The handsome god Osiris was Isis's husband. Together, they ruled Egypt with truth and justice. But Osiris had a jealous brother, the evil god Set, who wanted to kill him.

One dreadful day, Set succeeded. He held a great feast, and brought along a wooden box covered with the finest decorations. When his guests were relaxed at the end of their meal, he invited them to see whether they could fit inside it.

You can guess what happened next. The moment Osiris climbed into the box, Set slammed the lid shut, and threw the box into the River Nile. Osiris drowned, and the box drifted out to sea.

Isis was heartbroken—but determined. She searched everywhere, and at long last found her dead husband. But Set had been watching her, and would not let her mourn. Cruelly, he smashed the box and scattered the pieces of Osiris's body.

With great patience, Isis tracked them down and put them together again. Tenderly, she wrapped the rebuilt body in bandages. Osiris was now a mummy. She hoped his body would last forever.

But that body was an empty shell. Where was Osiris's life force? Where was his personality? Wise though she was, Isis could not bring her husband back to life in this world. She asked other gods for help, and they took pity on her.

Osiris was reborn and lived again, in the underworld. He became god and ruler of that dreadful—but hopeful—kingdom. Each year now, Osiris sends fresh grass and leaves and flowers from his kingdom underground. He brings joy to the land of the living—and, of course, to loving Isis.

INTO THE UNDERWORLD

The ancient Egyptians spent a lot of time and money creating splendid tombs for dead bodies. This was because they hoped that tombs would be homes where their loved ones could live forever.

Families paid for strong stone coffins to protect newly made mummies, and for artists to decorate the tomb walls with pictures of the gods. They made smiling statues of the dead. They left food, drink, and flowers to feed and please them.

WORDS OF WISDOM

At the same time, Egyptian people also feared that, unless they said the right prayers and performed the correct rituals, the dead person would never live again. So they recited spells to bring them back to life, and gave them copies of texts like the Book of the Dead, which they could use themselves in the underworld.

FINAL DESTINATION

Some myths said that dead people did not rest in their tombs, but flew up to the sky to become stars. Others told how the living dead went to the Field of Reeds, which was like everyday Egypt, but much better.

Egyptians also left shabtis like these in tombs. Their task was to carry out work that the dead person might be asked to do in the underworld.

MYTH LINKS

Compared with Egyptian myths, stories from ancient Greece described a miserable underworld. It was full of pale, muttering ghosts who slowly faded away as living people forgot them.

priest

mummy

priest dressed as Anubis (god of the dead)

table with offerings

family mourners

This painting from a Book of the Dead shows family mourners and four priests performing a ritual inside a tomb. Called the "Opening of the Mouth," it was meant to help a dead person eat, speak, see, hear,

TRUTH AND JUSTICE

Although Egypt suffered from wars and crimes, most Egyptian people admired honesty, fairness, and good behavior. They believed that even the smallest bad deed upset the balance between good and evil.

Egyptians said that this balance had been created by the gods. It was often pictured as a goddess, Maat, or as the Feather of Truth that she wore in her hair. Maat looked friendly—she was shown as a small, seated woman—but she had tremendous power. Any dead person hoping for everlasting life had to be judged against Maat by Osiris, lord of the underworld.

A TERRIBLE JUDGMENT

At the trial, the god Anubis took each person's heart and weighed it against the Feather of Truth. Thoth, god of writing, recorded the result. If a heart was light and free from lies or crimes, its owner could continue their journey through the underworld. But if a person's heart was weighed down with evil, he or she would be devoured by the terrible monster Ammut!

Osiris, wrapped in bandages like a mummy, watches over his kingdom.

MYTH LINKS

Osiris was often shown with green or black skin. This reminded Egyptians that he had died and been born again. Green looked like crops growing in Egypt's fields, and black was the color of fertile soil beside the Nile River. Both were welcome signs of life.

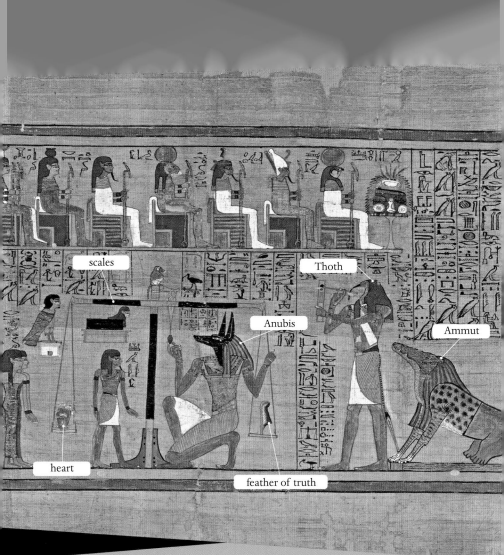

scales

Thoth

Anubis

Ammut

heart

feather of truth

WHO'S WHO?

With her crocodile head, lion's mane and paws, and huge hippopotamus bottom, Ammut was a very ugly monster. She was also the most fearsome. One snap of her greedy jaws, and a whole life was ended.

HOW DO WE KNOW?

It is over 2,000 years since the last pharaoh died. But just as the Egyptians hoped and prayed, their great civilization has not been forgotten. Their amazing statues, carvings, paintings, writings, temples, and tombs have survived, together with countless objects from everyday life. Most Egyptians today follow religions such as Islam and Christianity, but the ancient myths have not been forgotten.

SEEING FOR OURSELVES

Today, many people can go to museums to see mysterious mummies and many other fabulous treasures. They can read books and web sites or watch television programs and DVDs to bring the past to life. A few lucky travelers can also visit Egypt, see the pyramids, peer inside ancient tombs, and walk in the footsteps of clever, creative Egyptian people who lived long ago.

This is the entrance to Abu Simbel Temple, the tomb of Pharaoh Ramses II.

CHASING CLUES

Egyptian scribes wrote about subjects such as math, astronomy, and history. They also made collections of adventure tales and funny stories, and composed love poetry. But they did not write down Egyptian myths in a neat and tidy manner. We have to put together ancient Egyptian stories about gods and monsters from clues hidden in all the other evidence the Egyptians left behind.

Images like this painted tomb are some of our most important sources for Egyptian myths. By looking at them, we can learn what Egyptian people hoped and feared, imagined, dreamed, and believed.

MYTH LINKS

Many past peoples, such as the Vikings, believed that the world would end in a terrible battle. The ancient Egyptians believed that the world as they knew it would one day come to an end, with only Atum and Osiris surviving. However, they also believed that a new world would be created to replace it.

CHARACTERS, CREATURES, AND PLACES

Look at the words in brackets to find out how to say these Egyptian names.

GODS AND GODDESSES

Amun (Ah-moon) creator god, "the hidden one"; shown with a ram's head or as a king. As Amun-Ra, he was joined with sun god Ra to become Egypt's greatest god.

Anubis (Ah-noo-biss) god of the dead; shown with the head of a jackal

Atum (Ah-toom) ancient god of the Sun; shown as a king, with two crowns

Bes god who protected homes and families; shown as a short, fat, ugly man, with a lion's mane

Hapy well-fed god of the Nile River floodwaters; shown as a man with a big belly, draped in water plants

Hathor (Hah-thor) kindly sky-goddess; shown with the head of a beautiful cow. Pharaohs claimed she was their mother.

Horus (Haw-rus) sky god; son of Osiris; protector of pharaohs; shown with a hawk's head

Isis (Eye-siss) wise, loving, beautiful wife and mother goddess; wife of Osiris and mother of Horus; said to be the mother of pharaohs; shown as a woman nursing a baby, or as a woman with wings

Khnum (Knoom) craftsman, creator god; shown with the head of a ram

Nut (Noot) goddess of the sky; shown with her body covered in stars

Osiris (Oz-eye–riss) god of growth, fertility, and new life; shown as a mummy, with green or black skin

Ptah (Tah) god of crafts and craftsmen, also a creator god; shown as a mummy

Ra (Rah) god of the Sun, also called Re (Ray); shown with a hawk's head, or a crown shaped like the Sun

Sekhmet (Sek-met) aggressive daughter of sun god Ra; shown with the head of a lioness

Set god of chaos and disorder; brother of Isis and Osiris; shown as a monster with a long, beak-like snout

Sobek (Soh-bek) fierce god, created from Egyptian people's fears; shown with the head of a crocodile

Taweret (Tah-war-et) goddess who protected mothers and babies; shown as a pregnant hippopotamus

Tefnut (Teff-noot) goddess of moisture; shown with a lion's head

Thoth god of writing; shown with the head of an ibis

RULERS

Akhenaten (Ak-hen-ah-ten) pharaoh who ruled 1352–1336 BCE; famous for trying to make Egyptians worship just one god, Aten (the sun disc)

Alexander the Great brilliant army commander, born in Macedonia in 356 BCE. He conquered ancient Greece and ruled a vast empire in Asia and the Middle East.

Cleopatra (Klee-oh-pat-rah) last queen of Egypt (ruled 51–30 BCE); famous for her beauty, she used charm and cunning to try to stop the Romans from invading Egypt

Hatshepsut (Hat-shep-soot) female pharaoh (ruled 1473–1458 BCE). She built a wonderful temple next to her tomb.

Tutankhamen (Toot-ank-ah-men) pharaoh who died young (ruled 1336–1327 BCE); famous for the wonderful treasures buried in his tomb

CREATURES AND MONSTERS

Ammut (Ah-moot) monster from the underworld, who ate wrong-doers; shown with a crocodile head, a lion's mane and paws, and a hippopotamus's back legs and bottom

Apis (Ah-piz) real-life bull, worshiped at Memphis (one of the most important cities in Egypt) as a living image of the god Ptah

Apophis (Ah-poe-fiss) frightening snake monster

PLACES

Field of Reeds a paradise, like real-life Egypt, but better; one of the places where fortunate dead people might live after death

Giza (Gee-zuh) town on the west bank of the Nile River. (To the ancient Egyptians, "west" meant "home of the dead.") Giza is the site of three great pyramids and also the Sphinx.

Nile River longest river in the world (4,132 miles/6,650 kilometers), which brought life-giving water to Egypt

underworld kingdom of the dead, ruled over by Osiris

GLOSSARY

amulet lucky charm

astronomer person who studies the Sun, the Moon, planets, and stars

ba one of five parts that made a complete human. It is the form in which the dead could move back and forth between this world and the next.

Book of the Dead book of spells and warnings, designed to help dead people on their journey through the underworld

braided woven into plaits

canopic jar container for inner organs removed from mummies

civilization well-developed, organized society

hieroglyphs picture-symbols used by Egyptian scribes when writing about religion or royalty. Egyptian people thought hieroglyphs had magic powers.

inner organs lungs, stomach, intestines, liver, and everything else inside a dead body (except the heart) that was not muscle, skin, or bone. Inner organs were removed by mummy-makers, to stop dead bodies from rotting.

ka life force *see also* ba

mythical belonging to myths

natron chemical salt found in the Egyptian desert; used to dry out mummy flesh

offerings valuable gifts given to gods and goddesses. Egyptians hoped to receive favors in return.

pharaoh ruler of Egypt. The name comes from two Egyptian words that mean "big house," or palace.

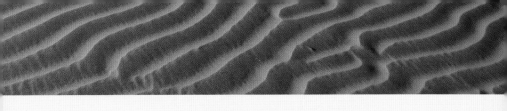

ram male sheep; a symbol of strength and fertility

resin gum from trees; used when making mummies

ritual special words and actions used when worshiping the gods, or when preparing a mummy for life after death

scarab dung beetle, common in Egypt; a symbol of new life, and of the Sun

scribe well-trained and educated person who could read and write. Few people had these skills in ancient Egypt. Scribes worked in temples and for pharaohs.

shabti little figure. Shabtis were placed in a tomb, to do any work expected from the dead person buried there.

shrine holiest part of a temple, where a god's statue was kept and cared for by priests

symbol sign, image, or sound that stands for something else. For example, a crown might be a symbol of a king or queen.

temple place of worship or home for a god or goddess. Egyptian priests presented offerings and performed other rituals at the temple to ask for favors from the gods.

underworld kingdom of the dead, ruled over by Osiris

FIND OUT MORE

BOOKS

Bell, Michael, and Sarah Quie. *Ancient Egyptian Civilization* (Ancient Civilizations and Their Myths and Legends). New York: Rosen Central, 2009.

Boyer, Crispin. *National Geographic Kids Everything Ancient Egypt.* Washington, D.C.: National Geographic Children's Books, 2012.

Elgin, Kathy. *Egyptian Myths* (Stories from Around the World). Danbury, Conn.: Franklin Watts, 2012.

Green, Roger Lancelyn. *Tales of Ancient Egypt* (Puffin Classics). New York: Puffin, 2011.

WEB SITES

www.bbc.co.uk/schools/primaryhistory/worldhistory/mummy
Find out how the Egyptians made a mummy.

www.bbc.co.uk/schools/primaryhistory/worldhistory/rosetta stone
Learn more about hieroglyphs and the Rosetta Stone.

www.britishmuseum.org/explore/young_explorers/discover/ museum_explorer/ancient_egypt.aspx
There is a special section of the British Museum web site for Young Explorers interested in ancient Egypt.

www.memphis.edu/egypt/timeline.php
You'll find a brief timeline of ancient Egypt at this web site.

www.metmuseum.org/collections/search-the-collections?ft=egy ptian&noqs=true
You can browse the Egyptian collection at the Metropolitan Museum of Art using this web site.

DVDS

The Ancient Egypt Anthology (The History Channel, 2012).

Ancient Egypt Unearthed (Discovery, 2009).

PLACES TO VISIT

The British Museum
Great Russell Street
London, England WC1B 3DG
www.britishmuseum.org
The British Museum has a gallery dedicated to Egyptian
mummies, statues, and carvings, and a re-created Egyptian tomb.

The Field Museum
1400 South Lake Shore Drive
Chicago, IL 60605
http://fieldmuseum.org
You can explore a re-creation of an ancient Egyptian tomb.

The Metropolitan Museum of Art
1000 Fifth Avenue
New York, NY 10028-0198
www.metmuseum.org
The Metropolitan Museum of Art has a collection of over 25,000
ancient Egyptian objects, including mummies.

FURTHER RESEARCH

Which Egyptian myth did you like reading most in this book?
Which characters did you find most interesting? Can you find out
about any more myths in which these characters appear? You
could look in the books or on the web sites given on page 46, or
even visit some of the places mentioned above.

INDEX